The BIRTHDAY PRINCESS Handbook

THE WOMAN'S GUIDE TO RECLAIMING YOUR CROWN

Linda M. Sacha

Life Support Press
East Haddam, CT

Published by Life Support Press
East Haddam, Connecticut

Cover art, book design and illustrations
Deborah Prater,
Image Access Design
www.IADonline.net

ISBN: 1-4196-1988-8
Library of Congress Control Number: 2005909929
Printed in the United States of America

This book is dedicated to
Linda Marie,
Champion for the Birthday Princess

...and to my mom, Donna; and my aunts Pat, Maryanne, Carol,
Charlotte, Della, and Mary. You always made us feel like our
birthdays were your greatest priority. I love you all, always.

Please give a hand to...

This is the official acknowledgement section where I list everyone who supported my project. I always check out these pages in whatever book I'm reading to see who the author thanks. Is it someone famous? Is their mom mentioned? Were they inspired by their pet beagle or a small child? What makes this person tick and to whom do they give credit? I think that tells a lot about the author's heart. It's like watching an actor's acceptance speech on an awards show—we don't really know who they're thanking most of the time, but *how* they deliver their thanks tells us whether or not we'd like to have them over to our house for dinner.

So this part of the book is huge for me. I have so much to be grateful for—and of course, I'm keenly aware that at this moment you're deciding whether to have me over for dinner. Actually, you'll know my heart very well shortly; right now I'd like you to celebrate these generous, loving people with me. As a writer, you humbly have an idea that you're eager to share, but it takes a village to get that idea into your hands. These players live all over the United States and their love and talents supported me in countless ways—from when I was lonely and overwhelmed to when I didn't have a clue about where to put a comma. So please put on your party hat and help me give a hand to...

The BP Board of Directors—Molly Lennon (college wonder-buddy and the original birthday princess), Roar Rowley (fab sister and fellow muse) and Anna Trusky (cherished sidekick, the BP editor general and so much more). You gals rock! From the first word to the last period you were my constant BP support team. You read, proofed, chatted, reacted, suggested, listened, and answered all the tough questions like, "Should the princess have a necklace?" You were in my head and heart throughout this entire magical process—how can I begin to thank each of you for your unique love and talent? Thank you, thank you, thank you. There, I did it.

Deborah Prater—illustrator and graphic designer—your talent and patience are exceeded only by your friendship. It was a dream come true to sit next to you as I created in my head and you magically made it all happen.

Nikki Sweet—you brought the BPH website to life with your talent and generosity, all enveloped in the embrace of our special friendship.

Arnie Warren—my dear friend and fellow author—your words of wisdom, thirst for creativity, and loyal friendship are a treasure to me.

My friend and "coach" Tom Welch—you were delivered to me in my hour of marketing need. Thank you for the motivation that only you can provide in your unique Tom Welch way.

SARK—the author, teacher, and inspirational goddess who, taught me the power of micromovements. By putting your brilliant principle into action, I moved The Birthday Princess Handbook, from "Yeah, I'll get that done someday," to consistent, small, forward motions that resulted in the birth of my dream. Thank you, SARK—I promise to pay it forward.

My amazing sister Jeanette Ball—in addition to offering great ideas, you provide me with daily inspiration of love and joy through the beautiful gifts of Jackie, Cathy, and Fred.

All my friends and family who supported me with their creative ideas and loving encouragement especially: Kathy Martin, Kris D'Errico, Linda Williams, Ira and Monica Sakolsky, Michelle Gaudet and Pat Thuman.

The multi-talented authors on the back cover who took their time to read my manuscript and comment with their hearts.

Birthday Princesses from around the world who bravely shared their birthday pains and pleasures with me.

John Sacha, my husband, best friend, and prince: Thank you for supporting me always, in all ways. You are a dream come true. ◆

Map to the Kingdom
better known as the Table of Contents

You Are Invited!

You are holding a special book. It's about you and me and women everywhere. It's about birthdays. It's an invitation to get in touch with your heart's true desires and celebrate yourself like never before.

How did you get this book? Perhaps you bought it for yourself because you already love your birthday and want to journal your memories. Maybe it was a gift from a friend who wants you to take pleasure in your special day rather than dread getting another year older. Or maybe something about it just piqued your interest and you want to know more. Whatever the reason, I'm glad you're here. Welcome to the fascinating journey of the birthday princess.

I began this project because I wanted to create a birthday journal for others that was more "official" and attractive than the spiral notebook I had been scratching in for years. I proudly created inspirational questions on beautifully designed pages. Then it hit me. If someone had given me a journal like this a few years ago I would have thought, "Oh, that's nice," and promptly tossed it in a drawer. There was a process of self-discovery that led to my establishing this precious birthday ritual. So in addition to the journal pages, I'd like to share with you my journey of becoming a birthday princess (BP)—a woman who has learned to cherish her day of birth. My intention is to wrap you in BP magic and motivation so that you will look forward to celebrating yourself each year.

Through years of disappointment, compromise, and growth, my birthday has evolved into an exceptional event. Along the way I wondered whether I was alone in my struggles and joy. I became intrigued with finding out how other women felt about their birthdays. Through a global BP survey and countless conversations with friends and friends of friends, I gathered secret birthday thoughts. I found some women who adored their birthdays and others, like me, who had been treating their day of birth as a second-class holiday. What they all shared, however, was that birthdays were a hot topic—a day we love to love or love to hate. All inspired me, and you'll find their insightful quotes throughout this book.

"I just love my birthday! I always think of that day as a new starting place, and get excited wondering what new happenings are in store for me." —K.P.

"I love the celebration but hate being old." —E.K.

"I hate my birthday but love it because it's such a paradox. Intellectually I know I am getting physically older, the signs of aging are beginning to appear—gray hair, creaky bones in the morning, menopause. But spiritually I have never felt better about who I am or about being a woman." —V.W

"My birthday is a time to celebrate, whether small or large, having lived another year, becoming wiser, stronger, and hopefully a little smarter." —M.C.

"Birthdays don't matter very much to me, although they probably should since it's the day I entered the world. I don't usually do anything in particular because I'd much rather do fun things as they occur to me than have to think up something special that is supposed to mean something on a special day. I'm neither pleased nor displeased with how they go because it's just another day to me." —S.R.

"I love it when my birthday rolls around. I couldn't be happier, really." —D.A.

"I don't have anything against birthdays or getting older, it's being the center of attention I despise. I feel badly that peole think they have to come up with a gift I don't enjoy receiving." —J.M.

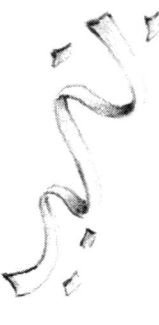

"It's not turning 49 or 50 that makes birthdays hard, but the attention that I don't like, that people for some false notion think I want." —S.D.

"My birthday is perversely filled with joy because it's my special day and I am loved, and it's filled with sadness because I acknowledge myself just once a year, kinda of like how you feel after all your Christmas presents are open. Now what?" —R.R.

"Am I pleased with my birthday? Seeing that it's just another day, I'm usually pleased." —M.S.

"My birthday is very impotant to me, and even more so with every passing year. Each year there is more to celebrate, whether a child's marriage, a new grandchild, new friends, old friends, another year on this earth." —S.J.

As I shared my BP journey with family and friends, an amazing thing happened: One by one, each woman embarked on her own personal journey, discovering her heart's unique desires and learning to relish the day on which she was born. Join me as we explore and expand on the idea of creating a day that's filled with what and who you love. It is a journey for all women who choose to love themselves as much as they love others—at least one day of the year. It is a chance to reclaim your crown.

My Story

The Birth of a Princess

The Birthing of the BP

I'm writing this sitting at a big wooden kitchen table in a cabin in the North Carolina Mountains. I'm alone in front of a fire and I've promised myself no phone, TV, or other worldly distractions. This is a first, I believe. It feels extraordinary to own my time and mind for four whole days while I take all of my whirling thoughts and bring them into some sense of order. I have so many ideas, memories, and stories about the BP journey that I am longing to share.

So, who is this Birthday Princess creature and where did she come from? She was born in my adult heart and imagination, fueled by a deep longing to recapture the birthday magic of childhood. I am a professional, mature, fairly sane woman who found that on many of my adult birthdays, I turned into an immature, somewhat irrational, disappointed child. My secret expectations for my gloriously special day were often unmet. My friend Molly and I would lament that birthdays just weren't as special anymore. I had slowly but surely shut down my birthday joy and muttered things like, "Oh, what's the big deal—it's just another day." Secretly, I was denying myself one of my sweetest desires—to be fussed over one day of the year.

"I like the way people look at you when it's your birthday. They know it's a special day and maybe wonder how you'll be celebrating. I love it all." —K.P.

9

When I was growing up, birthdays at our house were a BIG deal—or I should say they felt like a big deal to me at the time, and that's all that mattered. My Dad would wake me up singing "Happy Birthday" and ask me how I wanted my eggs. The night before, my Mom put together some treats for me to share with my class. Classmates sang, stuffed their faces, and treated me like their best friend. The nuns pinned a special badge on my uniform so that every teacher smiled adoringly at me, and the cafeteria lady gave me an extra cling peach on my tray. Life was good.

"I totally love my birthday. My mother and father always made a big deal out of it and I felt like I was celebrating the special experience of having been born me." —S.W.

I'd arrive home to find my favorite dinner being prepared (I'd chosen all the ingredients days before.) After the last morsel had disappeared, the front door would open, and aunts, uncles, and cousins would stream in to sing to me, eat cake, and bestow a present or two. By the time I collapsed into bed that night, it was crystal clear that I indeed was a Birthday Princess. I felt special—and it wasn't about gifts. Some years dinner was SPAM, the present was a coloring book, and the entertainment was a talent show starring my cousins and me. My father was a construction worker and money was often not abundant in the snowy winter months when my January birthday falls. Not to mention that I had to contend with the "post-Christmas lack of funds" issue.

Indeed, fancy food, expensive gifts, and dazzling entertainment were not the focus. I was. It was all about basking in the recognition that today was my day.

I was born and we were celebrating.

"Sometimes I get a huge goodie, other times we do dinner and a card. What I care most about is his fuss over me. Any gift is an extra." —M.J.S.

Hitting Birthday Bottom

Now flash ahead twenty years or so to adulthood. Family and friends are working ten-hour days, life is moving at a techno-frantic pace, and there are no cupcakes in sight. My husband arrives home and lovingly hands me flowers. "Happy birthday, Honey."

Hmmm. He remembered my birthday. Flowers are nice. This ought to be enough. Without fully understanding why, I slipped into the birthday doldrums. I repeated to myself, "What's the big deal? After all, birthdays are for kids."

Then I hit birthday bottom.

My husband was working out of town, I had started a new job, and none of my co-workers knew it was my birthday and of course I didn't tell them. My parents and sisters were on vacation and most of my friends just plain forgot. I never said a word. I wore my armor bravely throughout the day, and held my head with valor. As the day progressed, I felt myself slumping deeper and deeper into the thought, "Oh just grow up and get over this birthday stuff—it's darn selfish to expect a lot of attention."

I cried all the way home.

Questions began to race through my mind. How come no one made my breakfast? Why isn't someone baking a cake? Isn't anyone going to sing a little birthday song to me? Didn't I feel like a princess just a decade or two ago? Where the heck is my extra cling peach? When did I give up on all this birthday stuff? I love my birthday and I want it back!

"My childhood experiences of birthdays have a lot to do with how I feel about them now—they are charmed or special days where I am entitled to a bit more positive attention." —K.D.

With continued introspection and tears, it occurred to me that when we were children, most of us did not have to plan our own birthdays. Family remembered, teachers had it in their files, grandmas had it permanently burned in their brains. We just filled in the blanks as grown-ups initiated the questions: "What kind of cake would you like? Who would you like to have sleep over? Would you like hot dogs or macaroni and cheese?" I realized that if we don't have someone asking us those questions, we can easily slip into a mode of non-celebration. The little girl in me still had the same desires and expectations—I just didn't understand that I was now in charge.

When I got married and moved away from my family, I unconsciously assumed my husband would take over as birthday coordinator. This was the beginning of my birthday demise. Is my partner adorable, wonderful, and loving? Yep. Did he get the BP routine? Nope. Did I think he should have read my mind and psychically divined my secret desires? Yesiree. Did I pout, act hurt, and say I didn't care, for many years? Uh huh. Slowly, reality hit: Why should he know about this BP stuff—he was raised in an all-boy family that didn't make a big fuss over birthdays, and he dislikes being the center of attention! I came to realize that I was in charge of my birthday happiness, and it was my responsibility to ask for what I wanted.

Oh darn. This BP deal was going to take some real effort on my part.

"My Daddy sent me flowers for the first time on my 16th birthday and every year thereafter that he was functioning. So now that he is gone, I have taken it upon myself to make myself feel extra special like Daddy always did." —M.J.S., age 70

She's Back!

The thinking, crying, and "ahas" continued as I considered my previous birthday thoughts of, "I just don't have time to make my day special" or "I can't afford to spend money on myself right now." I also remembered what our therapist buddies Jim and Sari always said: "If you hear yourself using an excuse that involves time or money, then you haven't gotten to the real reason—there's something else."

Double darn. More crying. More thinking.

My "something else" emerged as a deeper issue of commitment, priorities, and most of all, self-love. I was pretending that it really didn't matter, when the truth was I had given up. I told myself that everything was fine in order to save myself from feeling the pain of shutting down my heart's desires. It was a clever tactic to avoid facing the truth that I had put my joy on hold, and I sure wasn't committed to myself. As women we can be gold medalists in this sport. Being anything less than ecstatic on our birthday is the first step in an insidious process of putting ourselves at the bottom of our to-do list.

We were born—that's worth celebrating. Period.

"As a child my birthday was not a huge celebration, so as a big kid, I have decided to make it the most special time. We extend the day to at least a birthday week, but I like a month!" —K.A.

Imagine saying to a child, "We won't be celebrating your birthday this year, Honey—we just can't seem to squeeze it into our schedule," or, "Sorry, no cupcakes—can't spend the cash." We would never deny a child these simple pleasures, yet we are so quick to deprive ourselves. We are kids in big bodies. There is a little girl inside each of us who yearns to celebrate her day. I believe that's why I chose the word "princess." It resonated with the child within me who was longing to feel special again. Not a selfish, prissy princess, not a demanding imp, not a spoiled girl from some fairy tale, but a woman embracing all aspects of herself at all ages.

"Sometimes I think the reason my birthday is not a big deal for me is because I usually try to make someone else's birthday a big deal. So I plan for other people's happiness because it makes me feel good. I really don't like focusing on myself, but maybe we should and make ourselves feel good, too." —K.F.

After much painful and joyful introspection, the result was, and continues to be, the official rebirth of the Birthday Princess. I tiptoed the first year and told my husband what I'd "kind of" like as a gift. I bravely dove in my second year and told everyone, "Tomorrow is my birthday—don't forget to sing!" And five years later for my big 4-0, I threw myself a fantasy party where everyone came dressed as someone famous they'd like to be. I then coasted nicely into "birthday weeks," saying to my buddies, "My birthday's next month and I'd love to celebrate with you. Want to go to the movies? Let's walk on Tuesday. I've got time for the park on Thursday after work."

Nowadays, if you call our house on my birthday you'll hear, "Hello, Birthday Princess Headquarters!" My friends and family know how much I cherish my birthday, and just like when I was a child, it's not about presents. It's about feeling elated, loved, and in charge of my own happiness. Not a bad present, huh?

"My celebration continues for as long as I can get away with it!" —D.M.

Yeah, but...

So that's my story.

Right about now you may be having one of several reactions to this whole Birthday Princess idea. Perhaps when you were growing up birthdays weren't a big deal or you don't have happy memories, so you may be having trouble relating to the idea that birthdays can actually be joyous or special.

One of my dear friends would get a stomachache each time I talked about the BP concept, and she couldn't face filling out the birthday survey. She felt anything but cherished on her birthdays while growing up. It was painful for her to think about never having felt like a princess before. At age 50, she's slowly beginning to celebrate her birthday and feel genuine joy. This is a courageous BP step, for she is proclaiming that she is willing to give to herself what she didn't get from others. It's never too late to seize the crown for yourself.

Maybe your birthday has gotten lost or diluted over the years. You've been way too busy being a wonder wife, partner, mom, executive, daughter, and the list goes on. No problem. This is an invitation to put yourself back into the equation.

Or perhaps you're saying, "What's all the fuss? I've always had great birthdays." Congratulations, you've been a princess all along! Now's the time to find new and different ways to pump up your pleasure and then enjoy recording all the fun in your BP journal each year.

"I am pleased with how my birthdays have gone. In fact, I'm looking forward to my next one." —G.C.

Here's the bottom line: If at the end of your birthday you feel anything less than 100% cherished, self-nurtured, and celebrated for coming into the world, it's time for a shift. Take a step forward from wherever you are...

RECLAIM it—if your birthdays used to be fun but recently they've been slipping away.

REFINE it—if your birthdays have been okay but you'd love them to be even juicier.

RECREATE it—if you've never had a great birthday, *now* is the time to make it so.

REJOICE in it—if you've been a birthday princess all along and just didn't know it.

"First I'd like to say that I prefer to have nothing normal happen on my birthday." —K.A.

"I've always tried not to make a big deal out of my birthday since there wasn't much family around and besides, that way you don't get disappointed. But last year my Birthday Princess friends threw me a party…sit-down dinner, a group of great friends, presents, even a pin that told everyone I was the birthday girl. And of course, a Birthday Princess crown. It was the best birthday I've had in a very long time. —D.P.

"Having breast cancer changed my perspective on birthdays. The more the merrier. I'm happy to be alive!"—M.G.S.

"On my birthday I normally celebrate quietly with my family, talk to my sisters, and thank my mother for the gift of life."—P.R.

23

Your Journey

Five Steps to
Reclaiming Your Crown

Going from crying in my car to answering the phone, "Birthday Princess Headquarters!" involved years of reflection, self-discovery, and refinement of what I really wanted. The process of taking a step from wherever you are begins by exploring these thoughts…

1. I want and deserve at least one special day a year.

2. It will be a pleasure to explore my heart's desires.

3. I am willing to act on my heart's desires and create a happy birthday for myself.

4. In an annual loving birthday ritual, I will capture my thoughts, feelings, and dreams.

5. I accept responsibility for my birthday.

Let's check them out …

I want and deserve at least one special day a year: I'm worth it!

For many years I was a corporate trainer. One of my favorite authors was Tom Peters, who wrote the best-selling books on personal and managerial excellence. Step one of the BP journey is best explained by a Peters' quote: "a blinding flash of the obvious." The decision to want and believe you deserve a great birthday is simultaneously huge and obvious. It's an obvious entry into the BP kingdom, and it's a whopper. It truly is the key to your heart. It's a willingness to proclaim…

I WANT to celebrate myself one day of the year and OF COURSE I deserve it.

It all begins with fully embracing this thought. That's the BP scoop. I love myself enough to create my day exactly as I want it. I was privileged to have been put on this earth today, and I'm going to surround myself with the people and things I love.

"It makes me feel wonderful that people are happy to celebrate the day that I was born because I am certainly thankful for it!" —S.M.

I was recently flying out of Florida and found myself seated next to a friendly, professional-looking woman named Connie. She told me she had been working there and then had taken some time to herself. As we exchanged career stories, I discovered she was a mom and a very successful business owner. When I told her about my BP project, she burst into tears. It turned out that her "time to herself" was an escape to a condominium to celebrate her birthday alone.

She explained, "My birthdays as an adult have been so awful that I dread them every year. Everyone deserves to be recognized on their day, but no one understood what I wanted and needed. I couldn't worry anymore about what people were planning or not planning. I decided to take care of myself." Connie cried even harder when I told her that she had begun her induction as a Birthday Princess. With immense courage she had taken the first and hardest step in becoming a BP—deciding that she wanted and deserved a special day.

Enhancing your self-worth is not an overnight process—it's a life-long commitment that begins with one new loving thought about yourself. When we embrace this first step, we are daring to proclaim what the L'Oréal gal has been telling us for years: "I'm worth it."

What would your birthday be like if you were 100% behind yourself?

"It occurred to me that birthdays are one day of the year that bring into focus how you feel about yourself the other 364 days of the year. If your cup feels empty all year, it's not going to get filled up on your birthday." —N.B.

It will be a pleasure to explore my heart's desires: What exactly DO I want?

On the next few pages there are questions to spark your thoughts for discovering and recording your heart's desires. These are the ever-so-important pages where you pause and ask yourself, "What do I really enjoy?" Sometimes amidst the wackiness of life we don't stop long enough to think about our "favorites." You've just been granted time and space to focus on yourself for a moment and become the designer of your birthday.

Every woman's pages will be very different—what is dreamy for one princess is a nightmare for another. Each will have a unique definition of "celebration" with various comfort levels for hoopla. I have learned to honor and appreciate others' diverse needs and enjoy celebrating their unique desires.

"A birthday cake is not necessary, and there is never any singing or any other scene at the restaurant. That is how I like it." —D.M.

"On my birthday I try to get other people to spoil me...shower me with gifts...buy me dinner, sing. I want attention!" —R.R.

After completing my pages I had a realization that changed all my birthdays to come. I was indeed longing for an "extra cling peach," AND I wanted to share it! When I looked back at my childhood birthdays my joy always involved some type of celebration with others. How amazing to discover such an important ingredient that I could use to create happy birthdays for myself. I am finally at peace and no longer feel selfish about the fact that cards and flowers left me feeling like something was missing. Just like when I was a child, presents are not necessary, just share a piece of my peach with me and I'm in BP heaven.

So what will *you* discover? On the pages that follow, dare to record your hidden joys and passions. Once these are completed, they become your template for creating your annual birthday celebration. Your list will be added to, erased, and adjusted as you change throughout the years. You also won't be squeezing everything on your list into one celebration. Exploring and identifying your heart's desires simply means you've thought about yourself, and now have a full basket of goodies from which to choose.

To really embrace this task, how about an uninterrupted meeting with yourself in a favorite spot? Would you like to put on some music or light a candle? You're stepping into the pleasures of your heart…

Heart's Desires

Initial date of recording: ....

    Over the years as you revise or add, use different colored pens and date your new thoughts. It's fascinating to see how your desires change over time.

    Begin by reflecting on your childhood birthdays. Record a typical birthday celebration at your house growing up. What did you do? How did you feel?

_____

_____

_____

_____

_____

_____

_____

What was the most favorite part of your birthday as a child?

Do you wish it had been different in any way?

Reflect on and record your recent adult birthdays and how they've felt to you.

How are your childhood and adult birthdays the same? different?

39

As a result, what would you like to adjust about your current birthdays?

Do you believe you deserve a fabulous birthday of your choosing? Why or why not?

Favorites:

My all-time favorite…

Home-cooked foods:

Restaurants and specialties:

42

Desserts: _____

_____

_____

_____

_____

_____

_____

Special edible treats: _____

_____

_____

_____

_____

_____

Types of activities: _____

_____

_____

_____

_____

_____

Places to go: _____

_____

_____

_____

_____

_____

_____

Kinds of entertainment:

My people quotient: privacy, a few friends, a big celebration?

 Friends and family that I'd like to celebrate with:

My definition of celebration: ⟡

Great gifts for me:

Birthday "musts"—what is your "cling peach?" (the main ingredient to ensure your birthday joy):

_____

_____

_____

_____

Birthday "must nots:"

_____

_____

_____

_____

_____

_____

So, if you were going to create your ideal birthday in this moment, it would look like this…

Thoughts I have about myself and my birthday, after completing these pages…

_____

_____

_____

_____

_____

_____

_____

_____

_____

_____

_____

Now you know EXACTLY what you want!

I am willing to act on my heart's desires and create a happy birthday for myself: I'll do what it takes.

You know that you deserve a great birthday, and you've uncovered the things you most enjoy—now it's time to create a plan of action. This is where you get to ask yourself, "Am I willing to either do what I want for myself or ask others for what I want?" This is a step that can take time to fully unfold within you. It's centered on the profound concept of doing what it takes to create your own joy, a skill that can feel foreign to many of us.

When thinking about doing what you want, the word "selfish" often floats into the picture. This is not about satisfying a selfish whim—rather, it's meeting a need that is an integral part of who you are. When a plant needs water, you provide it. When the cat is hungry, you feed it. When your friend needs a hug, you hug her. So when you discover what makes your heart sing, why wouldn't you give it what it needs to start singing? Your heart's desires are the very fabric of who you are; of course you want to be sure they are nurtured and met.

*"My birthday is my day. I don't want to have to
remind anyone of it or give any suggestions
as to what I want as a gift or celebration."* —K.P.

As far as asking others for what you want, you may have heard yourself say, "If I HAVE to ask, then just forget it." Why would you want to help orchestrate your birthday? So you get what you need and desire. Why should you have to? Well, you don't—as long as you're pleased with how your birthdays have been going. If you'd like your birthday to be happier, then take the leap and ask for what you want. If you don't speak up, not only is it unfair to yourself, it's unfair to the people in your life who either *assume* you're happy or *wish* you were! I have discovered that the people I choose to be with on my birthday are pleased to enjoy my joy.

Which gal would you rather hang out with—one who walks around smiling because she does what makes her happy and has a full cup for life, or one who mopes around with an empty cup and wants you to guess how to best fill it up for her? Not only do I want to be friends with the first gal—I choose to be that woman and I'm certain you do, too.

*"My mother says that she looks forward to
buying me presents because I'm the only sibling that
provides her with a Christmas list for my birthday!
I take away her anguish and keep in the fun for her."* —D.M.

52

My husband was thrilled when I recently created a mini-notebook for him called "Guaranteed." I filled it with entries that guaranteed his success in the BP arena! It has the names and numbers of the services I love, like dance classes and massages, along with my clothing sizes and favorite stores. I also included many of entries from my heart's desires pages and of course, my "cling peach"—a celebration! I asked my husband if he was insulted to get a list.

"Insulted?" he replied. "I don't have to guess anymore and have your birthday be something that I dread because I'm sure I'm going to fail. I never knew how important a celebration was to you. I think every woman should do this and then talk about it with their loved ones. I was clueless—why didn't you tell me this stuff sooner?"

Hmmm–why didn't I tell him sooner? Oh, let me list the ways…

    a.) I didn't know it myself.

    b.) I thought I *was* telling him through all my years of whining.

    c.) I thought I didn't know how to ask.

    d.) I thought I was being selfish and demanding.

    e.) I thought he should just "know."

Well there you have it in a nutshell—all of the original reasons for writing this handbook! It's also why "doing what it takes" can be so full of growth opportunities and may take time to fully embrace. As I look back I see how I have grown into being able to express my needs and ask for what I want.

Let's explore asking for what *you* want. Requests are not bossy or demanding; rather, they're things like…

* Time with you is important; I'd like to meet you for a walk on Tuesday.
* I was thinking lunch would be fun; I've wanted to try that new place.
* Birthdays are a big deal to me, so I'd love a phone call from you that day.
* Will you plan a get-together for me this year? Surprise me!
* I'd prefer to have a private birthday this year—I've got my own special plans.
* I could really use some new body lotion.
* A cake would be great—the whole office can celebrate.
* Please plan something low-key this year, I'd like to sit back and relax.
* I'm in the mood to go out and dance!
* No need for presents, but I love cards.

"I celebrate my birthday for seven days.
I tell everyone it's my birthday week!" —K.Q.

Here's one of my BP agendas that I asked for and then arranged. For starters, I took the day off and then several days ahead of time, orchestrated the following…

6:00 time alone to do BP journal
7:30 walk and breakfast with girlfriends on the beach
9:00 facial and massage—alone!
12:00 lunch with buddies
2:30 shopping with my gift certificate that I asked for from spouse
5:30 favorite dinner with hubby at home
8:00 meet friends for dessert and music

As you can see I really packed it in. It was a unique year with limited time so I experimented with squeezing in ALL of my desires. After years of refining, I've realized that a combination of celebration and private time stretched over a few days gives me the greatest joy. Your treats no doubt look very different. The point is—YOU examine. YOU choose. YOU orchestrate. YOU enjoy.

"I take charge of my birthday if no one else does that year. It does not matter whether I plan the fete or someone else does. I know what I want so why wouldn't I create it for myself?" —E.D.

My friend Molly is a longtime BP, so I am always eager to hear her birthday plans. I was unprepared for the answer she gave one particular year: "Oh I don't know, I'll just see what I feel like that day. No big deal." BP alarms shrieked in my head—she was slipping down that all-too-familiar slope of birthday mediocrity. She had been through a year of personal change and wasn't feeling up to her usual celebration. We talked for a while and began making plans that resulted in a superb birthday rescue on her part. She chose a quieter celebration because it reflected her current needs. SHE chose, rather than it choosing her. Aaah, the sign of a true princess.

So whether times are challenging or life is grand, love yourself enough to put some advance thought into your day. We would never say to a child the morning of her birthday, "So what are you thinking of doing today?" Give yourself that same consideration. (To discover what other BPs around the globe do to celebrate their birthdays, visit www.thebirthdayprincess.com.)

My sister Jeanette read this manuscript, and as she finished the last page she looked up with a gleam in her eye. I love that gleam because it usually means she has something profound to say. I was right.

"Okay, you've got me. I'm inspired, and I get that I'm in charge of my birthday happiness. I realize that I want my birthday to be a little different than every other day of my life, but I don't know where to begin."

Her BP older sister smugly replied, "That's why you've got the Heart's Desires pages."

She further explained, "Okay they're important for introspection, but while I'm growing into this, I also need a down-and-dirty birthday checklist. Now that I'm motivated I want to be quickly coached into action!"

I heard my sister's "do what it takes" wisdom, and I'm all for providing multiple options to ensure birthday success. So may I present to you, on behalf of Jeanette…

56

The Birthday Princess
Do What It Takes Checklist

Put a check mark in all that apply! You can make copies of this page to accommodate your ever-changing desires.

1. What are you in the mood for this birthday?

- ☐ laughter
- ☐ contemplation
- ☐ learning
- ☐ privacy
- ☐ joy
- ☐ personal growth
- ☐ celebration
- ☐ inspiration
- ☐ intimacy
- ☐ motivation

2. What ingredients sound appealing?

- ☐ food
- ☐ the outdoors
- ☐ party
- ☐ adventure
- ☐ pampering
- ☐ the arts
- ☐ travel
- ☐ exercise
- ☐ shopping
- ☐ quiet conversation

3. Who do you want to celebrate with?

- ☐ friends
- ☐ loved one/partner
- ☐ strangers
- ☐ family
- ☐ myself
- ☐ like-minded people

4. What kind of dress sounds appealing?
   - ☐ comfy
   - ☐ casual
   - ☐ costume
   - ☐ formal
   - ☐ dressy
   - ☐ business

5. How are you going to make it happen?
   - ☐ organize it myself
   - ☐ call a friend
   - ☐ discuss it with loved one
   - ☐ check in with family

When you look at all your check marks, what kind of celebration is emerging?

The BP bottom line is to do what it takes to create a great birthday that's just the way YOU want it. Do it with your signature—the only guideline is your joy.

"Since I got married 28 years ago I have planned my own birthdays and told my family what we were doing. A few years ago I decided to make them more exciting for me— so I planned things like hiking, white-water rafting, skiing, and horesback riding" —M.J.

"I like spending my birthday alone,
but usually my family takes me out for a hectic dinner
that is not a lot of fun." — V.W.

"When I have a birthday I celebrate for a whole week
which I start out by preparing a luncheon for my lady friends.
It's also a time for deep soul-searching as I realize
I must carefully plan these remaining senior years." —I.S.

"The first time I kayaked was at a 60th birthday party for me,
planned by me." —E.D.

" I have started indulging myself with a special treat.
This year my friend and I are getting facials and then we are
going to see Tina Turner in concert to really celebrate." —S.M.

59

In an annual loving birthday ritual, I will capture my thoughts, feelings and dreams: The Birthday Princess journal

Ritual: a ceremonial act.

Isn't it a superb idea to have an annual ritual of reflecting on and recording the key thoughts, dreams, and events of your year? The world stops for a moment while you contemplate and privately honor yourself. It's a history of you, recorded and witnessed by you. Each time you update your BP journal, you demonstrate to yourself that you and your life matter. It is your annual tradition of capturing your inner thoughts on your day of birth.

The BP journal invites you to reflect on and celebrate the past twelve months and dream about the upcoming year. You record your birthday celebrations and how the BP journey is affecting your life. I love going back and reading my past entries; it's amazing how our lives and priorities shift as we grow. It's even more amazing to feel and live the effects of it all.

"My birthday is a day I try to do some reflection about my life and where I am. How has the last year been? What significant accomplishments have I completed and what am I planning for next year?" —L.P.

"My birthday is a time where I reflect on my parents and how thankful I am to them for having me and all the sacrifices they made." —M.C.

There are five years of beautiful pages designed for your annual journaling ritual—take a peek on page 73.

It's all about you. How can you go wrong?

I accept responsibility for my birthday:
I own it.

Whether you loved your last birthday or it was less than perfect, make sure to give yourself the credit either way. One year you may have a day that's peaches and another may be the pits. As long as we take responsibility for our day we are still claiming our lives. Responsibility does not imply blame but rather embracing your "ability to respond" to what's happening. If your birthday was lousy, look at what contributed to the lousiness, and learn from it. If it was fabulous, celebrate how you contributed to its fabulousness. Either way–own it!

Why own it? Because we are not victims in our lives—we are victors. We have the amazing ability to continually look at how we contribute to both our successes and our less-than-successful life events. It's taking hold of one's scepter and owning what you create. It's an amazing feeling.

I have found that some years do indeed require greater flexibility and creativity than others. When the kids are little, parents are sick, or careers are demanding, we adjust, but we don't give up completely. We get to ask ourselves, "How can I still make this a special day for myself? What is one small thing that will fulfill a piece of my heart's desire?" Some years it may be as simple as a warm bath. As long as you are willing to accept your own choices, you're in charge of your own joy.

"We evacuated for Hurricane Floyd and got home the day before my 40th birthday. We had been in a friend's warehouse and it was like Noah's Ark. I am allergic to cats and I woke up with a major headache and nausea on my big day. No one called to say happy birthday because they were all being hammered by Floyd. My husband rapidly pulled a family dinner together at our house and called me at 4 pm to ask me if I could vacuum because we had company coming. I know my 41st will be better!" —S.M.

"One year I was working on a disaster job on my birthday. They gave me the day off and I rode the emergency rescue vehicle so I could see the people we were helping. That was a memorable birthday." —M.J.

A few years ago my birthday was looking a bit shaky—I was seriously considering ditching my BP commitment. My husband was wildly sick with the flu, my sisters were across the country, my parents were celebrating in heaven, and we'd moved many states away from all my BP cronies. I got cards. I got calls. I got a couple of e-mails. "Shouldn't that be enough? This birthday is just going to be different," I heard the old familiar voice chime in. I took a deep breath. Okay, several deep breaths. Was I willing to settle and abandon my heart's desires? How could I salvage this birthday and create the celebration I love in some small way? The princess in me adjusted her crown. "This year is different, yes—hopeless, NO!"

I ventured out into the snow to a new deli and chose a beautiful meal to go. As I perused the dessert counter I couldn't believe my eyes. There before me was my all-time favorite childhood delight: homemade, not instant, butterscotch pudding. It had been 20 years and there it was, the dessert special of the day! I came home, warmed my dinner, poured my husband some ginger ale, put a candle in my pudding, and asked him to sing with me. He was thrilled by my willingness to take charge of my own happiness and his ability to help me do so when he was feeling so helpless. I was exhilarated that I had carved out a slice of joy for myself on a less-than-perfect day.

That was a close call and a true test of my commitment to myself and my birthday happiness. There will continue to be additional growth opportunities, but each time the learning comes more quickly and it's a lot more satisfying.

"One exception to a happy birthday was when I'd been in a relationship for 13 years and she happened to leave on my birthday. That sucked but it didn't ruin birthdays for me. She was the problem, not the birthday!" —S.W.

"You asked me if I was pleased with how my birthdays were going, and when I think about an answer of "no" I'm reminded of the joke about the man who complains every day about his homemade lunch. Finally, one day after hearing enough of his complaining, his friend asked him, "Why don't you ask your wife to fix you something else for lunch?" The man replies, "Oh my wife doesn't fix my lunch. I do." We get in life exactly what we choose! So if I am not pleased with my birthday. I know who gets to change it!" —L.S.

So accept all the credit you deserve if you've created a day that's worth remembering—one way or another. Accept. Adjust. Grow.

67

The Icing on the Cake

As I reflect on my Birthday Princess journey, I realize how much I've grown and how terrific that feels. My friends and family have now joined as official creators of BP events for me and for themselves. I found that as I have celebrated myself more, it has offered others the invitation to celebrate themselves more. There's a whole lot of crown swapping and plain old happiness going around these days.

The icing on the cake is that my husband and the world now live with a woman who is happy with herself and her birthday. He no longer pales at the thought of trying to guess how he can "succeed." I no longer act like an unhappy and confused child. I am a partner who co-creates my day with him. After he read this manuscript he looked up with tears in his eyes and said, "I get it. I really had no idea."

He had no idea. In that moment I knew I had possessed the crown all along and all I had to do was reclaim it for myself from myself.

The year I celebrated my 50th birthday was downright spectacular. Several months before, I sat down and really thought about how I wanted to honor this milestone in my life. I arranged private time with my husband and major girl time with my sisters. I spent time alone writing to four mentors, thanking them for the tremendous contributions they made to my life. I planned a celebration with friends and family and asked everyone to bring their favorite food. We danced in the living room as my friends' band played my favorite songs. I also fulfilled a lifelong fantasy of singing with a band (I can sort of carry a tune). I bravely belted out "Man I Feel like a Woman" by Shania Twain and grinned through the entire song. Each woman at the party, as well as my girlfriends who weren't there, received a homemade present and a letter of appreciation for being an amazing woman.

At the end of it all I sat down and grinned from ear to ear. The little girl who longed to share her cling peach was basking in her happiness. Someone commented that I had gone to a lot of trouble and asked if I minded creating my own celebration. It was so easy to reply, "I loved every second of planning and creating my happiness." In the last twenty years I had slowly but surely reclaimed my crown.

It's funny—once you're really immersed in your heart's desires, you begin to realize how good it feels—and when you're not honoring your true wants and needs, there's a void. It's downright addictive; an addiction to self-perpetuated happiness. Choosing and creating your heart's desires one day of the year is great, two is even better, and weeks are just plain divine.

As I continue to grow in self-love, I realize it's the greatest gift I can give back to the world. One who chooses to cherish herself, to reclaim her crown, has the gift of love to share with others.

I share with you the glorious Birthday Princess. May she always dance freely and joyfully in your heart.

Who is a
BIRTHDAY PRINCESS?

I am a woman who loves myself enough to...

➤ believe that the day I came into this world is a day worth celebrating.

➤ stop and think, "What do I really want on my special day?"

➤ take at least one day of the year and completely immerse myself in my heart's desires.

➤ know that whining gets old and gets me nowhere, and that self-creation gets me everywhere I want to go.

➤ be courageous enough to put my fears and pride aside and ask for what I want.

➤ realize that friends and family love participating in my special plans, knowing I'm doing exactly what makes me happy.

➤ know that I have the "ability to respond" if my birthday is anything less than delicious.

➤ close my eyes at the end of my special day, smile, and think, "That was superb and I deserved it!"

➤ fully embrace that reclaiming my crown is the greatest gift of love I can give myself and the world.

The BIRTHDAY PRINCESS is indeed a glorious creature who has come to learn that she is the beloved princess of her own kingdom.

Your Annual
Birthday Princess
Journal

planned for no interruptions?

how about your favorite music?

are you comfy?

Happy Birthday!

Year _____

Welcome to year **1** and your crowning initiation.
Long may you reign! Enjoy your time with you!

Highlights of my past year: _____

_____

_____

_____

_____

_____

_____

_____

_____

_____

I celebrate my accomplishments—big and not so big:

The qualities and talents it took to reach these accomplishments:

I am especially grateful for:

Some of the challenges I faced and I'm more than alive to tell about:

Intentions and dreams for upcoming year:

I deserve this and more because:

_____

_____

_____

_____

_____

_____

_____

_____

_____

_____

_____

Read page 71, "Who Is a Birthday Princess?" Journal your thoughts and feelings on which statements feel comfortable and which are currently growth opportunities.

What are your Birthday Princess plans for this year—and if you've already done them—how'd they go? Have you considered your heart's desires on page 35 or the "Do What It Takes Checklist" on page 57?

Photos, sketches, or other birthday memorabelia

planned for no interruptions?

music?

candles?

Happy Birthday to You!

Year _____

Welcome back to the chronicles of you!

Highlights of my past year: _____

_____

_____

_____

_____

_____

_____

_____

85

I celebrate my accomplishments—big and not so big:

The qualities and talents it took to accomplish this:

I am *especially* grateful for:

Some of the challenges I faced and I'm more than alive to tell about:

_____

_____

_____

_____

_____

_____

_____

_____

_____

_____

_____

Look back on page 79 and read your intentions for the past year. What are your thoughts?

Intentions and dreams for upcoming year:

I deserve this and more because:

_____
_____
_____
_____
_____
_____
_____
_____
_____
_____
_____
_____

Read page 71 and journal on your thoughts of how your BP-ness is feeling this year.

_____

_____

_____

_____

_____

_____

_____

_____

_____

_____

_____

_____

What are your Birthday Princess plans for this year—and if you've already done them—how'd they go? Have you considered your heart's desires on page 35 or the "Do What It Takes Checklist" on page 57?

Photos, sketches, or other birthday memorabelia

are you
comfy?

no
interruptions?

any
other
treats?

Happiest of Birthdays!

Year _____

Congratulations—you are committed to celebrating you!

Highlights of my past year: _____

_____

_____

_____

_____

_____

_____

_____

I celebrate my accomplishments—big and not so big:

The qualities and talents it took to accomplish this:

I am especially grateful for:

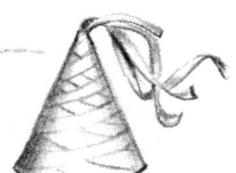

Some of the challenges I faced and I'm more than alive to tell about:

Look at your intentions and dreams for this past year on page 91. Did things happen as you intended?

_____

_____

_____

_____

_____

_____

_____

_____

_____

_____

Intentions and dreams for upcoming year:

I deserve this and more because:

_____

_____

_____

_____

_____

_____

_____

_____

_____

_____

_____

Read page 71. How are the BP statements feeling this year? Journal
your thoughts.

What are your Birthday Princess plans for this year—and if you've already done them—how'd they go? Have you considered your heart's desires on page 35 or the "Do What It Takes Checklist" on page 57?

Photos, sketches, or other birthday memorabelia

planned for no interruptions?

music?

treats?

Happy Birthday to You!

Year _____

Highlights of my past year: _____

_____

_____

_____

_____

_____

_____

_____

109

I celebrate my accomplishments—big and not so big:

The qualities and talents it took to accomplish this:

I am especially grateful for:

Some of the challenges I faced and I'm more than alive to tell about:

Look back on page 103 and read your intentions for the past year.
What are your thoughts?

Intentions and dreams for upcoming year:

I deserve this and more because:

_____

_____

_____

_____

_____

_____

_____

_____

_____

_____

_____

Read page 71 and journal on your thoughts of how your BP-ness is feeling this year.

What are your Birthday Princess plans for this year—and if you've already done them—how'd they go? Have you considered your heart's desires on page 35 or the "Do What It Takes Checklist" on page 57?

Photos, sketches, or other birthday memorabelia

120

all set for private time with yourself?

Happy Birthday!

Year _____

Congratulations on continuing to journal and celebrate yourself!
What has gotten you to this point? What's different?

_____

_____

_____

_____

_____

_____

_____

_____

_____

Highlights of my past year:

I celebrate my accomplishments—big and not so big:

The qualities and talents it took to accomplish this:

_____

_____

_____

_____

_____

_____

_____

_____

_____

_____

_____

_____

I am especially grateful for:

Some of the challenges I faced and I'm more than alive to tell about:

Look at your intentions from last year on page 115. Journal your thoughts:

Intentions and dreams for upcoming year:

Plans for this year's celebration:

_____

_____

_____

_____

_____

_____

_____

_____

_____

_____

_____

_____

Journal your thoughts on how BP-ness is feeling and how you've grown.

_____

_____

_____

_____

_____

_____

_____

_____

_____

_____

_____

Photos, sketches, or other birthday memorabelia

Time to get a new journal to continue celebrating <u>YOU</u>!

132

© 2006 Deborah Prater

About the Author

Linda Sacha (her friends call her Sacha) was introduced to her princess self growing up outside Buffalo, New York. A woman on a lifelong quest to know, love, and trust herself fully, Sacha is fiercely committed to supporting others on the same path.

In addition to being an author, Sacha is a heart coach and an award-winning voiceover artist. As a professional speaker and seminar leader, she has dazzled thousands nationwide using her humor and wisdom to help people embrace their inner talents and build better relationships. She also had the privilege of teaching learning disabled students, serving as chief training officer in a financial institution, and acting as communication director of a nonprofit organization dedicated to healing hearts through the arts. Although Sacha's common career thread has always been to pay attention to heads and hearts, there was a time when she was also devoted to feet (she owned a Swedish clog store.) She has a bunch of degrees but her lips are sealed.

A recovered birthday pouter, she lives in Connecticut with her prince and their amazing rescue Chihuahua, Trixie. She's wacky for gardening, constant learning and being a member of the improvisational troupe Comedy on Demand.

Sacha looks forward to hearing your Birthday Princess feedback and stories. Please visit her at www.thebirthdayprincess.com.

Contact Us!

Please visit **www.thebirthdayprincess.com** to...

- Purchase additional Birthday Princess Handbooks
- Share your own Birthday Princess stories with women around the globe and
- Find out about book signings and speaking engagements with Sacha!

Have a creative project in mind? These fabulous women will help you make your dream a reality with their professionalism, joy, and extraordinary talent.

Cover design, illustrations, and book layout—Graphic Genie
Deborah Prater
www.IADonline.net

Editing, creative writing, and marketing copy—Word Angel
Anna Maria Trusky
amtrusky@aol.com

Web Designer—Cyberspace Queen
Nikki Sweet
www.upyourbusiness.com

316472

Made in the USA